The Humor In Everyday Living

By

Annette Stovall

ISBN: 1-4033-7930-0 (e-book)
ISBN: 1-4033-7931-9 (Paperback)

This book is printed on acid free paper.

1stBooks - rev. 11/1/02

Dedicated
to those
who love
humor how
it comes.

Contents

Selective Grins On You Know

Putting The Grin Between You And Me

If Not Day In Summer Jests

by

Annette Stovall

The Year In Summer

A Teen's Vindicated song—

Hooray for school is how I'm free

To go along here ballgame season.

But one big blooper I just can't see

Is I go look for a job.

July 4—When mothers less for inside chores do rather want the leisure Independence Day bring firecracker blooper.

Split seam blunder—When this summer mom rips her dress swift in the chase for little Mike at a picnic.

A tired sponge—The mom too tired for campaign-drive if stays with in summer yard racket.

"Peep holes too small"—What fat Johnny said after bent his thumb on the just hung tree-house.

Summer Press Conference—When July the 9 year old calls a meeting with 2 parents and requests for more time watching television.

Late August—When some parents fed up with his 12 year old antics feel he's right for the military.

End of summer—For some juveniles the end of Dodger season.

One Summer When It Was a Right Occasion for Try Anything…

…traipsing on tanner tile floor a few summer turns, it didn't look dingy afterall.

…tinted the gray hairs covered wasn't bad one day.

…writing at the desk one bright afternoon went fine when mate didn't ask her to pick up blade and weedtrimmer in town.

…she tested a first occasion wore pink hot pants

…riding a bike first try with slips gave a child thrills.

…a summer toothache gave splendid occasion for try Ambisol.

…lounging in old pajamas he picked from rag bag and game is on tv went dandy few times his wife didn't kick.

…it was grand year for try ridiculous pastime.

…sitting in with mate watched sports on tv, not eccentric dull one month.

…test blue waters by the beach went splendid swell for the mom of 6 children.

…losing weight wasn't wrong just for wear a size 8 tan belt.

Remembering When It Was An Ideal Day…

…mom didn't have fit over here spring cleaning went ideal.

…hair was next blowing in air was ideal for the wind-swept look.

…it didn't next dark storm up a breeze because of no umbrella, child's rain hat or scarf on a picnic…an ideal day.

…you looked between the mirror and shape was ideal.

…your mate got government job wanted. Ideal for his age.

…you didn't begrudge a smaller government house your family next living where was that way out for enjoy ideal in country weather.

…mom was glad she donated 'ideal' to the Salvation Army.

…you didn't begrudge a spring day ideal for fruit drinks.

…anyday was ideal for received a huge government check into hundreds even under dark clouds.

If You'd Make a Wish for a Better Holiday

Easter Wish—that the weather would be perfect for show your frock in the Easter Parade.

Wish at Mother's Day—that the family present of a suit would fit right and won't tag hips where she added 3 inches cellulite.

Desire for Father's Day—that the automatic thing the children gift of this year would come equipped with things like batteries.

One Labor Day Hope—that the 2 in-laws would become friends since now the yard picnic extolling cake, salads and plenty of meat just for them.

Mom's Halloween Urge—that a rare treat they hand the child would be coupons better than trick candy.

A Thanksgiving Wish—that here by the turkey 2 in-laws won't squabble like they did last year over who'd make the better wish Thanksgiving Day with break the wishbone.

Desire for Christmas Day—that all the gray-white snow and presents greatly make you happy could be enriching this year overmore better than year before.

Designs on Love Will Fit When the Occasion Rhymes

At a beach Sandbox—Where a younger son in bliss designs a kiss.

Affection Hope chest—Where the too-shy-son keeps a hope but. shied of ask a dreamboat out.

Oodles Telephone call—What a school-age teen will hear if styled from a love is clear.

Case of the Stairs—When a teen says he never stares, but next eyes her pretty mod-skirt up the high school stairs.

Line on Parent Blues—When the well-meaning tad turns her mother-love blue with designing mud on the rug.

Misnomer Errand—When he brings the spring day-drinks her quarts. But love instead wants quartz!

Admiration darts—What they greet on the spring park-seat.

Pleasant Recall on file—What a June bride keeps at home. But she admits album is big because wed inside adornment took long.

If you go Back To a Good Ole Day, It Won't be the Same

Why go back to a same ole neighborhood if won't be the same?

If you travel back to a same ole street corner, way it's now constructed won't be the same.

It won't be the same one construction crew used if they tearing down or building.

The once good ole brick house resided in—it won't be the same if new shop replaced it.

After search for old yard shed took six 2-by4's, two rows of nails and hammer twice to repair—it won't be the same if they scrapped it.

It won't be a public stand for newsrack the same—once for easy access for you read the personals while people stared on.

There'll be a policeman on the block superbly rides his travels won't be the same.

There'll be the needed 2 to 3 fire-hydrants up and down the street, but a local fire-house 8 blocks away won't be in the same place.

Remembering Back to That Summer

There was little surprise if…

…the car ran out of gas on the way.

…nobody in the car could tell where park gate's entrance was.

…mom neglected bring an extra blanket and water cooler to campsite or outing but brought an ice pick along nobody needed.

…they all forgot how 10 million bugs run rampant on a picnic.

…parents forgot how many burgers 6 children love to eat.

…a few times mom remembered bring the family umbrella, rainhats and scarf. But no dingy colored skies next for storm owns the field trip.

…a hubby got lost on the way to campsite.

…the 5 year old fell behind canvass tent trailer one night while sleeping.

What a Different Mother's Day Card Would Say

Dear Mom,

I wish you cheers on Mother's Day. And from now on you won't have to pick up socks from the floor after me.

I promise. From a son.

To a Special Mom,

Here' s to the only mom I have won't let me not do a homework.

From a smarter daughter.

To a Dear Wife and Mother'

Yes, you are for surprise. And I have you to thank for saying just. 8 days ahead what microwave oven surprise package you'd like!

From your husband.

For a certain Daughter.

A red card is for the red roses faded. I hope you send a better present this year.

From a mother is hopeful.

Mm to Mom,

Bunch is for family group like at my house unless this year they do different like take you out for a grandest evening.

From a friend.

Mom's thanks to the Family.

I'm supposed to be cheers on Mother's Day. And the new dishwasher gift you all chipped in on is delightful. But pink sorrel won't match my kitchen.

From Mom.

When They're Single People Playing it Safe...

…one cool daughter at home won't agree to Monday wash heavy loads not unless mom irons on Tuesday.

…this cool 20 year old gladly will agree two take the blade mower and dead electric saw in for repairs only if his dad won't screw directions.

…only a thinking person won't acknowledge class reunion to 'bad one' 'til safe after others 'fess up.'

…one widow mom won't hire a baby sitter 'til known her child won't be snatched.

…one big teenager will take the sitter's job after ask, "What's to eat in the frig?"

…a smooth bachelor's reason for not snap at rude boss he only day one rented an apartment.

…it's a clever son lets his dad win the argument because he's safe from paint a shed Monday.

…one spinster lady won't go long without wear a fake wedding band allots she's not up for grabs.

Concerning if He says...It means

If he says...

"Is that the fare in sleepwear?"

It means...

He thinks you'd look great in a negligee.

If he says...

"Of course, you can turn down the covers anytime, simple thing like that."

It means...

He thinks you should sit through he sips Pepto Rismol while glimpsing through the paper.

If he says...

"Of course, it's your mother was on the verge. Who else this holiday had a floor yawning?"

It means...

His mother-in law hinted too much about being sluggish while his wife fought. With cookout flames in the yard with Labor Day

If he says...

"Even on a holiday some ad's in the newspaper about six kittens."

It means...

One cat having 6 kittens is a bit much.

If he says...

"Why should you be always reminding me take the car in?"

It means...

Of course, he'll take tie car in for brake, wheel and oil check but not this minute.

If he says…

"I would watch tv, but…"

It means…

It's too late to watch the ball game.

If he says…

"But, dear, couldn't it wait a while yet?"

It means…

He doesn't think much of buy the set of tree lights, candles and ribbons this early in September.

If he says…

"Of course, 3 children love their grandparents here no matter what."

It means…

He hopes 2 in-laws don't repeat visit all day, not until November

If She says…He may Agree or say Different

If she says…

"Let's look thru the map."

He may say…

"Not now, dear, while I read the Sports Column."

If she says…

"Of course, we should inspect through. It's for our next vacation spot."

He may say…

"Of course, but not now. Once every few years enough trip taking anyway."

If she says…

"Isn't it near time for King's birthday celebration?"

He may say…

"Darling, you know it comes every year one month or the next." Or else, "The wall calendar won't say?"

If she says…

"I learned today in my refresher's class a man Otis invented the elevator. Did you know that?

He may say…

"Is that a test?" Or else, Didn't you know? My memory's even better than 6 years ago."

If she says…

"Why do you Summertimes say, I need to take a mower blade in for sharpened next or else should buy one lb. of nails, ladder and 6 rolls of tar paper for the shed on Monday?"

He may say…

"I know. You think I laze. That or weather just not."

If she says…

"Dear, I'll get the suit from the cleaners in town. You forgot it yesterday."

He may say…

"I prefer tire went flat. While you're at it, you can have the cat washed and brake fluid checked."

If she says…

"Dear, I still think good time for check the map."

He may say…

"You would think that." Or else just nod.

You Know Summer Camp-Out Time is Here When...

...6 o'clock early a.m.—the family readies them for go camp-out.

...3 members load tent and gear but forget one last hall item that mom ducks in for.

...7 o'clock a.m. the next morning—five will arrive just in time see how bright summer rising over National Park grounds.

...2 parent's first with raise a camp-out tent don't have a quip but "Did we pitch it right."

...12 o'clock noon—one parent and son on a hike in the woods won't miss of abandoned old. house.

...after the family mutt along wipes dirt on one smaller daughter, she just shrugs it off.

...evening afternoon—one back from on a hike, son this eager displayed 2 splendid colored rocks he boast found them in the abandoned old house.

...after mom brings a fishing reel, instead, they'd rather stick with pig in a can!

...9 o'clock at night—the parents build a campfire while listening to crickets ri-vet, ri-vet sounds liven up things among the bushes.

...here, parent don't have to relate to 2 children why camping out is

Summer Games—Do They Ever Play Out

Aunt Sally is Dead

Memory states of back then unless you feigned how illusion aunt died, she wasn't dead.

Ring-Around-the-Roses

The summer game your child might still remember play it better than 'do yard work.'

Hide and Seek

The game you're child has 0 recall how you played it with—boy seeks out a kiss.

Simon Says

Unless they act out some simple directive, lad and lass counted out won't think "Raw deal," if turn to mom's cook out or something.

Volley Ball Discovery

That the ball pitched early on at school tosses just as well recently between June and July.

Below Sunset Find

That a streetrace at summer begins 8 p.m. or 9 no later.

Divergent Double-Dutch

Below your day it's a rap different since daughter does it like on tv the 'rope queen.'

The Pun in Ball Memory states it was all in fun whether you played it with friend or alone.

The Ball in How You Play the Game

Touchdown Tour de Force

Better academic game if C student brings home A instead.

Major League Skill—When the hubby picks the Mets versus Dodgers on TV over dine and movie spree—the other game.

Class Room Fiasco—Pro amateur's ball makes 'class instead of in the schoolyard basket.

A Run Tour de Feat

A deed score connected if daughter of age 12 clears away every dish. If she scrapes dried egg score a feat home run.

Acrylic touchdown

Where the slipped folly cup makes goal.

College Bestframe

The gameful out of state college your freshman picks over military plebehood.

In Pane's dead center—Where active fly ball drives the hole in one.

Housewife's Strike-out

One summer month when rest of family in with tv baseball and leaves mom stranded in the kitchen.

What A Different Father's Day Card Would Say

To a special pop on Father's Day, this gift comes with best wishes. I hope it makes you smile. From your eleven year old.

To the ideal father I'll ever have says, "Yes'," to let me stay up the extra hour on weekends. From your youngest son.

A father is for surprise, allowance is what I saved, and first payment is made on the boat. Now we 2 can own the wishes we want. From a teenage son.

Satisfaction is words in a card comes with a little pink address book. I wanted to give you something else but what satisfies? You don't like pink ties! Love from a wife.

This card is for a fun dad loves to take pictures. I hope you bring me of 'em in to work. From a boss.

If you ask me I'm pleased for this one day I get the glorious praises and a package won't work without batteries, I have to laugh. From a laughing father.

Dealing With Single Person in the House

Parents hesitate over where daughter in strength wants the item picked up—cleaners on the corner!

Any parent may frown where the child is grown up tossed the socks on the floor.

A father won't know why a strapping son ditched motor blade from chop the lawn unless he's next evading rays.

You give in to where the 20 year old spent last night hence breaking curfew.

One couple debates when a bold son hates to nail and hammer in the yard job says, "It won't college ace!"

It makes a pair grin of frank son says living at home at his age 21 hedges on 'bachelor'

You try explain to adolescence daughter what old maid for, thirtyish she doesn't rank.

Parents may listen to what the 15 year old's question. Although they won't agree to, next, date in a theater without one parent along.

What's New On Breakfast Terms Etc.

Capital Yolk Disaster—When one egg missed the plate christens Poppa John in his Elk suit.

Scrambled eggs Alias—At Wanda's house they don't call 'em all scrambled but coddled.

Designated Term—If breakfast looks odd it's because it added something announced like French crepes.

Stir-Fry Order—At breakfast grandpa amuses with instead of pancakes he craves stir-fry grits!

Basket Car Case—Semester's crowd they rate for stuck in 2 seater like eggs in one basket.

Occasion had her toast besides—If parents allotment made her glad, she at sophomore brunch with no chaperon besides teacher at far end.

Bringing the bacon home—Term for he'd rather bring check home than get drunk.

Fresh-air-juice in the noggin—What one track team member dubs for he infrequent hastes to school if skip eat.

Teen Slang—If at age 16 stuck with chaperon, it's like egg in the face.

Meal-Time Is Seldom Prime-Time To Eat

Chow-time Gambol—When the wee tad takes meal-time to mean flip-his-airplane time at the table.

Gimme-Gimme-Gimmick

When your 11 year-old wants the apple and orange fruit at breakfast mealtime, but only he wants em' for later the school-class-party.

The Trick in Table-Feedback

Just as her 2 year-old says 'no' to eat at mealtime mom's cheeks turn red.

Calorie-count Game

Nobody over age 15 to eat above 200 calories a meal ahead they eat in a Banquet hall.

Dr. Boner says

Don't expect your months-old child to eat a full dish a meal of carrots just because you urge.

Mrs. Pretikin for Ice Cream says

If the vitamin brand appetizer doesn't work, scoop any-flavor stimulates.

Early-Fudge-Brownies—What child with a knack against oatmeal wants at 8a.m. breakfast!

Concerning Things Did Happen Routed On Vacation

The car battery went dead behind they started.

On vacation route about a mile into next town, he got his directions crossed.

It was 20 to 30 miles between journey and trip city, end driving for when 4 children tired of cramped up began flailing stick balloons out the car window.

On trip road their 8 year old wanted touch the farm animal's cute baby cow too far off the highway.

Now inside trip city's gate, his wife obsessed with urge to tour they passed eleven blocks back city's wide monument.

In the city's hall he checked for more directions.

On the trip he found the roadside vegetable stand okay but missed the campsite by a mile

He didn't know the price of gas could be high in smaller city.

Concerning Things Did Happen on a Wash Day

Monday morning breakfast one daughter did get burnt on kitchen toaster.

At noon her 3 year old did dump good bowl of soup on the floor.

Later her husband requested she'd pick up tools, nails and spray paint from Hardware store. But she did only go washing.

A friend was in the Laundromat did have to mention she got that catalogue item wanted. The one with all the push buttons.

She thoughts the Laundromat janitor wouldn't notice she went from 3 to 5 pounds fat Holiday weekend.

She did have to be clumsy enough to splatter bleach over delicate smock.

She did have to out of car gas money when she just brought enough for 5 washloads.

Having Fun With
There's A Rule In Any Case

by

Annette Stovall

Just As A Rule

To err is flowers turn unnatural pink and brown placed the sun too long.

To break a crocus vase almost is because I'll catch it on average carpet

Haste makes waste since I'll get a sore joint, talc on my shoes and clothes ripped just for do things ordinary at home

If my mother rules against keep the same blue suit it's because I'll only wear until it bags.

Early to bed early to rise true if due in average Clinic room long wait.

Two will go to Carnival if rule is eat Largely pink cotton candy.

Rule on dinner stain is if the pin-stripped silk turns faded of the greens, you'll know 'valuable less' for top vogue.

To err is not divine if 2 Pre-schoolers will forget you've only 2 hands the maximum.

To say "Give a hand" may stir a tired husband if after you'll ask the minimum 3 times.

It Comes To Laying Down The Law

Television law—I wouldn't miss what comes or Prime Tv come heat or icicles.

Law on ride a bike—I would correct my grandchild with, "In the living room's no place for it."

One neighbor's law—It was easier to bake 3 pastries on Sunday for the Seniors Group Social than if she had waited Monday she'd have missed 3 Tv soaps.

Youngish gown law—The sooner our daughters agree we're not over age for wear one, the better off we'd feel.

Law on Friday the 13th—Even at my age I would be skittish about do anything.

Freshness law—I would urge my 2 grandchildren who'll visit with the longer they're up with 4 Tv Sitcoms the less fresh for Tuesday school.

Husband's game law—It's easier if here learning early what his laid down law is. He watches the game through—short of other team would have to be winning.

Greeting Cards. Some Rules About When

I love you card. It should be given any day by either mate.

Birthday card. It should be given with the gift before a mate picks on how many 35 years are in the candles.

Happy Anniversary card. It should be presented in the room's full of guests and a friend's 3 man combo when even if she is wearing the now off white dress.

Best wishes at age 40. Given now before other indication's newest pimple, he or she responds may add the equal thanks.

Get well wishes. It should be handed with the fruit before who gets well to say "I don't like apples."

The morning joke card. It won't hurt it says "We both need slimming butter waistline down.

Card to a grandmother. If the mate honors her now 50 gray years will add words behind what the card stated with the gift—it may add him big kiss. to a grandmother. If the mate honors her

As A Rule On A First Date

Occasion if he gives a designer's card he'll at least be charming.

If he brings along the flower bouquet he'll think that's better than to address next her's a dull smile.

Like 2 darling mothers ever will advise, they do go smartly dressed.

Respect for evening meal at Diner's Ballroom deserves a couple even if his 20 years old will tip with just a quarter.

Compliments are in order though he may will wait for the moon standing rises when he tells her, "You look pretty tonight."

She'll hear if he says "Let's take a drive" even if a Gas Station card's low.

A rather solution is either she'll rather shake hands at the door or otherwise distinguish to go abode inside.

In the end he hopes a first evening date went smoothly they'll remember.

Since It Comes To Every Occasion

I'd Rule Out on…

…picking up behind the children every occasion. You'll just be doing their job over.

…clearing out what they should in any case. If the children are big enough for in home chores they even have your strength.

…tell the children where leave muddy shoes and boots every time. If they really love you they'll remember where if times you skip.

…habit of butter up the mate's boss every turn. Smoother words won't even score for bigger Christmas Bonus.

…keep every appointment on time. You'll have to wait the full hour in Doctor's Office anyway.

…meet with the gals for Banquet Speechmakes everytime. You'll just be taking notes and overeating is all.

…being always first to apologize. If a friend was in on dispute it had to have 2 people.

…always relating to the Grade School teacher, "Child is a brainstorm." It'll say so on report card or not.

Rules On The Special Couple Will Chat

The special couple will share the light chat in the living room where he watches football.

The special couple will share the bicker's chat on the couch if they both end up remained speaking.

The special couple will enjoy each other's company saying the words at home or in public. "I love you" in the chat.

The special couple would rather cry on the shoulder than don't say I gained 6 pounds.

The special couple won't believe every word a mother-in law may next horn in.

The special couple will relate to little surprise chats on the phone between two—the mate at home and other on the job.

The special couple will both tolerate grins bringing it up about whose hobby watched gameshows day before.

Some Protocol Answers to D's and B's

Delightful Liaison—It's okay if one partner wants an affair if 'who with' comes up spouse.

A Dad Blasted—What one marriage partner ever gets him in the hassle.

Bluff Solution—The answer to if the partner only bluffed "No" to gift a 'class ring' to son is yes.

Quick Alumni Defense—When the Class Alumni says "No" to after Prom night Reunion go drink and drive.

Affirmative Data—It's true one night owl mate took the money rap's 'Despicable Restraint' for what his out put had.

Students for Pep Meet Disport—When that many students entertained for an in school's auditorium, some are glad for no smoking allowed.

Better Etiquette—When the daughter won't miss a mod belt if she gave to the Salvation Army.

Briefed on Dog in the house—The small house won' t hold of 5 cute little kittens where the youngster wants dog instead.

If We Rule In Favor If Early Spring

First day of spring—If it does come early, I'll celebrate with take the first spring walk with you in public.

On Easter We'll rule in favor of spring nice for big hat won't appear overmuch in Easter Parade.

On Memorial Day—We'll expect our favorite spring day for ribs on the grill but won't want a sudden rash of storm may drive us inside.

Graduation Day—When they present it in the spring auditorium you'll tell your High School senior "You look lovelier, here, in white," and she won't next say it's idle chatter.

One principle day—The earlier Monday you start a spring cleaning chore the later in the attic. And all because it's principle warm day for spring cleaning or take a spring holiday.

Every morning—I'll know definitely rule is early spring if the bird's keep boosting celebration with songs chorus the yard around at Sunday thru Monday.

One beleagured day—Besieged with overworked or on perimeter I'll let sprinkles on leftovers go bust, but I won't let a good spring feeling go to waste.

As A Rule About Notes

Dear dad,

Thanks for the Ouija Board clue about Father's Day almost here. Though you'll still have to wait on a gift.

Your 12 year old son.

Dear family,

I could urge a rule that simple honors I receive on Father's Day would praise me thru the week, but I don't.

From the hubby and father.

Darling husband,

As a rule you may realize the little time we spend together is on a holiday, birthdays and Sunday. You keep through Saturday.

Wife of who works too long.

Dear Joe,

This note's in your pocket reaffirms it won't matter how you might spend your bonus this year. But don't rule a vacation for two.

A loving wife.

Dear dad,

I taped this note on the bathroom glass only because mom told me. Happy weight-in dad.

Your eleven year old.

Darling sweetheart,

I forgot I'll be tired after work. Count me out on bring home 6 half pint tins kitty menu from the market, but rule me in on sample each 3 dozen cookies you'll make for the Bake Sale.

Hubby Al.

According to What She Says… It Means

If she says…

"Let's watch television."

It means…

They're not going out for the evening.

If she says…

"Dear, I like your trendy haircut. But is that any way to do?"

It means…

While in his favorite chair just loafing his hair is gone messy tossed up.

If she says…

"Dear it's that time. A present day husband should help out with house-chores."

It means…

She feels it's a man's job to empty trash, wash dishes and change dirty diapers.

If she says…

"Of course, it's not role reversal. You only watch the children on one or two weekends.

"It means…

To her he shouldn't be intimating put a strict curfew on little free time she spend out lollygagging with gals from women's League. If she says…

If she says…

"I'm not in this at all."

It means

It's ok if presently the guys pop in while he loafs in baggy pajamas and old scuff shoes. But don't drag her in on the tiff.

If she says...

"Why do you always have to be right? Like about the screen. It's hot and the files come in."

It means...

She's right about the screen. He should have taken it in to Hardware instead of patch it up himself with cardboard.

It she says...

"Of course, it should do vistarama too."

It means...

He can look to buy a new television set.

Things We Wouldn't Like To Be Without

We wouldn't like to be without a washing machine. We'd never get a wash load bright.

We wouldn't like to be without a dyer turns our average clothes gorgeous fluffed up. Prettier than were.

We'd hate to be without a refrigerator keeps our turkey, salad and other holidays' repast elegant fresh is right above spoiling.

I'd hate picture to be without a colored tv set wouldn't show the picture on vcr.

We'd hate to be without our grand kitchen stove. We wouldn't have a stove for cook a feast.

We'd hate to be without garbage disposal takes our ham and other tough bones if we could find that model.

I wouldn't like to be without a gorgeous stand up vac's just right for sore joints.

We wouldn't like to be without our colored sheets. We wouldn't shed the soil better.

On Your Pees and Ques at Age Over 40

It's highly unpolite to seek less than large artifacts at any 40ish function.

Taking pomp in extant age reunion means they're all present and deserves in over 40's limelight.

Plausible query is what a teacher at reunion suspicions may heard about he was going bald.

Act my age was easy between night out with friends at a time Dinner Party was practical.

Anniversary is not inquisition time on early years perfect but how so many middle years possible.

Prod the Photo Album for a one last over 40 face is quaint but fun.

Prod the mid-life crisis—birthday next in over 40 qualms.

Primitive Yearbook—there's no best place for add a 40ish note.

Errors You Rule In On Summer Vacation

Fourth of July Error—You know it's here, summer vacation, when the 12 year-old in error pops a firecracker too loud for senior's ear.

Summer slip up—Picnic in the yard it's no excuse for your 9 year-old slipped up to say too many "It was an accident."

Blunder before depart—You missed make the family's reservation and right at the ticket line it dawns on you.

Blunder on the trip—Just when family arrived in the hall at State Monument your daughter of 5 years, now, says, "I wanna go potty."

Case of Mistaken Identity—It's by the Art Display when strangest lady you don't know of mistake occurrs will say "Don't I know you from somewhere?"

Blooper on the Field Trip—Just because you missed bring a top-notch cooler along, the sun reeks havoc on family thirst.

Blot on back yard Campout. After the mutt bumps from juice outside the tent, junior gets a grape blot on togs won't wash out late.

August with the flaw—After on the porch beneath sun's hot rays you feel the flaw in August.

Defining Rule in First Semester for These You Can't Stop

The average rule—Getting up early semester". And after shake the child hard letting him sleep the added hour.

The route commandment—The father demands he drive the child this 1st semester before change that to first week.

Law of first week preliminaries—The teen reports semester at Albana High involved paper work better than at one school his pal took a longer I.Q. test.

Semester jitters—You can't stop your own tears when your 5 year old says "I wanna stay home."

Last minute request—It's 8 seconds before the school bus arrives when your 12 year old needs a dollar for the ice cream and cake they're having first semester party.

The common assumption—What it likely will cost, he'll have to walk, run or bikeride news delivery for semester's ball-game uniform.

Legal quip at first semester—Anybody near semester's class can't help the hearing "Same teacher I had, only she's 20 pounds heavier."

Grade logic—You don't believe anyone can beat your child's best grades first semester.

About Habits I Wouldn't be Surprised if...

…Miss Philips has a habit of tug her skirt before eat a feast.

…that uncle has a habit of show up in time to spoil terrific occasion when you plan the quiet dinner party just for two.

…one teenage daughter has a habit of hoard the telephone just when you need it.

…her 10 year old's bad habit is walk his mud sneakers all on the rug.

…her months old baby's got strangest habit of hold his breath instead of keep crying.

…her date's worse habit is wear a coat out of vogue kilter with nicer 6p.m. dress.

…one gal won't even consider 'on a blind date' without she interrogates habit compares other 'out' occasion notes with 3 friends.

…Old Mrs. Grundy has the funniest habit of put spice in her coffee pot.

When It Comes To Sticking With The Chat

I Wouldn't Rule Out on…

…chatting over stick with a diet after 'pinched 3 inches fat hips' revealed in the mirror.

…chats about 2 more arriving than invited to small dinner. Including that uncle with bad jokes.

…it'll take more than 2 jokes to cheer 2 in-laws with Family Reunion. But it only takes 5 minutes chat livens up a child.

…morning wake-ups to tune of 3 kittens. Then in the chat saying, "They're not mine."

…conversing with friend on the phone say definite, "Don't chat long because today Friday you shop sales."

…hearing my grandmother's chat say "Extended age mellows Senior outrage becomes norm." Though she does get fed up on aches.

…chats about the 5 o'clock bus 'tied up' when you need to get home quick.

…as your own chat foretold, you added 2 inches stomach with Thanksgiving.

Defining the Rule in Winter Beside the Snows

Law-of-lateness by a mile—If pop drives the son the added mile to school in dead winter snows, he can't stop next of angry boss scorn.

Demands on early-to-rise—The earlier Friday mom starts her canning for Local School's Drive behind the snows, it still won't be time for Helen's chat may call.

Made-to-wear-formula—We instruct the child "Enter at kitchen tiles better than snow melts on the carpet."

The out-hill recipe—Somebody's child always asks to go sled riding because the hill's fixed with snow, rides, and giggly friends.

One evening rule—Just because dad was out late Sunday doesn't mean he won't try out a new snow plow on Monday.

Proverbial howls—Once Rover leaves the house he's next for broadcasting how much winter did really snow.

Rights to a snowman—Everybody's child wants one. And some blow your mind with toys just to hear say "Okay."

The reason why we hover—We can't help behind the snows we near the warm vent or fireplace is better.

Middle Age and Feeling Confident

If I tote the shopping bag over 3 blocks, I'm like who youngish age recedes but prevailing.

I don't have my daughter's youngest skin, but I still can't resist have the marmaladed entree.

If I rather go to crowd's middle-age celebration and wear brown, brown suit, brown effects, it's alright I'm middle age.

At my age my eyes are dim, but, decidely, I still take the down staircase

I don't bother with spending 50 dollars for black suede's just another black hat.

In the shop I have the feeling I'll take the novel print suit where miscellany on display. I may look odd but different.

I don't worry that a teenager will yell over khaki I scorched since children are all grown.

I'm convinced I'll make it 'side folk other my age, wrinkles are the crisis, now started on middle age.

Selective Grins On You Know

by

Annette Stovall

You Know You're Keeping Fit When...

...you don't mind broadcasting to a friend you went from large size 12 to 10 took only 3 months.

...going thru small outfits in Dress Shop, it won't make you feel fat.

...if somebody compares you to your mother looks young you take it better.

...you don't complain to members at the gym after lift of 5 lb. weight, "It's too heavy."

...somebody mentions pass the mashed potatoes and gravy at Banquet's dinner hall and it won't make you wish for 6 pounds thinner.

...you're less afraid of weigh on the scales for dread of gained 3 pounds.

...even a quiet mate comes out bragging how prettier you look.

...glancing at page after pages' skinny fashion model doesn't make you wonder when you were that size.

It's Called Cheating Yourself When...

...after hand over big check to Supermarket chain you for-get Bank Account's overdrawn.

...soon after seeing appeared to be old friend in Thrift Shop you neglect a cheery "Hello."

...before the garage sale you wanted things. Then behind buy little gizmo odds and ends, they weren't that extremely useful.

...if you let a friend be convincing on fix the stereo between minutes with one pair pliers and screwdriver. It never works if something electric gone wrong.

...you pay overtime for in the Parking Lot because today's last minute appointment ran extreming unusual.

...you try at fix 'small job' yourself 'til after botched it up have it fixed in Repair Shop's better afterall.

...in public you read the ad columns near-sightedly because in public seems conspicuous for wear glasses.

Knowing When We're Down On Our Luck

Last week I didn't mind the rent was up 'til shop in Supermarket reminded how much.

Monday I didn't mind if lazy cousin slept over 'til after he broke with vow didn't look for job on Tuesday.

Reality is saving coupons by the month. Contradition is not every corner market duplicates trade-in.

We mind the overdrawn draft. It's a myth 'til we need to borrow from a friend compelling things like pick, ice or screwdriver.

Check the Personals ads any month now is the norm 'til next connect with right bargain.

When you don't get much in the bargain you know inflation still.

We don't go to Doctor's office without a thought for same average exam our way of thrift in mind.

We don't hasten to get another credit card when we owe overmuch on one.

Comparing our living to a friend's is tradition 'til re next realize have to get by on less income.

When savings won't last a rainy day through you know for into life's storm.

It's A Different Point Of View With But I Know

A Fun Selection of What Some People say

"Of course, he does have ridiculous ways, but I know my particular brother."

"True, my students complain times about least little thing. But I know they'll written exam do Alien Vespertine Types without a gripe.'

"Dad said same thing this morning. I already know, you think it's for my own good."

"But I know it took us 2 hours 15 minutes to arrive at Speaker's Auditorium. But drive back we absolutely won't be 90 minutes driving."

"As advertised house none for Grand View Plaza. But people think twice before kiss off a bird bath display. I know I would."

"Admittedly it either should release candy or coins."

"Course a wife shouldn't bring Anniversary present into it. But better this way I remind you what today is."

"Certainly they are darling kittens. But knowing our father six darling little kittens still need a home."

"It's either meant for cellar or garage, but in the living room's no place for a pinball machine."

You Know You're in the Hole Debtwise When...

...in the middle of August you still make the minimum payment on Christmas giftspending.

...you pay less heed to your child wants money for ordinary tasks in summer school because sounds only ridiculous.

...you shop the stores for quality becomes any brand of soap. spray cleaner and 4 rolls paper towels instead of 4 stacks.

...this low on funds you buy any brand green peas mostly.

...each time you have in mind get the 400 dollar luxury item instead you remind self of 100 dollar limit.

...during the week you don't flatter your mate with a rare surprise package because instead you bought yourself a smaller trinket.

...you don't argue with any weekday now may have your innovative spirit for do it yourself jobs.

...4 kittens at home have to wait supper because they don't know for how you shop around for different rated brand of pet food.

Knowing When To Be Less For Show-Off

If I were you…

…I wouldn't show off the new item in the house if your neighbor just frowns upon the mention.

…I wouldn't reveal the next fun mother-daughter secret if your daughter won't smile.

…I would introduce my hubby in dirty sneakers to guests in the house. But I wouldn't reveal the junk pile where he picked 'em from.

…I wouldn't show off the new shoes just make my feet hurt. Not while standing in Clinic overcrowds line.

…I would tend to brag if child's a Track Star. But I wouldn't next hooray he's no Honor Student.

…I wouldn't show off the new china, silverware and micro-wave oven to who neighbor's just been informed of 'On the Welfare now.'

…I would donate to Salvation Army. But not before giving first picks to who you know on Child Support.

…I wouldn't put the unwanted words in on couple who argues if I were the mother-in-law.

Knowing Your Decorations And Ornaments

Since there will be a teen's decorated C card she insists on repeat, "I did at least pass the school year."

This mother will seldom chasten response with, "Better next year" since studious daughter brings home ornamented essays top grade mostly. What few others try or care to.

Since he'll go in swanky tie escort decorates flash to Prom night expect anything for Class Reunion.

Behind she starred her voice on the phone said "I'll see you" she didn't expect within the hour.

One auntie will defend 'Latest model' no matter how the ornaments change.

If at last an uncle drops ornamenting of guilt nephew after he smashed the car he'll only foretell, "Boy deserves to pay from his allowance."

Not until the teenage charm'll outshine party guests, then, you recognize him.

Since she'll beaming eyes one famous reason for miss a movie it'll likely be blind dating.

Knowing When It's Time To Take The Signal

If you hate on waxed floors the shine ran out you don't always buy more.

If washdays you hate 'ring around the collar' you know old way doesn't always work.

If appointment day you dread it makes Clinic line extends because you need ex-rays, lab tests and hard raps on the knee, it's time to go anyway.

If grass is cropped always greener on other side fence, what probably needs reversed you living pitiful.

If you waiting Friday's uncharming, in Dental Office with your daughter's probably crowded.

If you hate bought a toy fake place of child's real mutt more cheerful, you know you're on the low budget's Welfare.

If every month with steady looking for your train to come in you need the Welfare raise or Job Chore.

If you don't like you get the papers bi-monthly anymore, you don't storm the corner stands bi-weekly.

If you didn't buy the dud thing it's because you know it was a doosy.

You Know Spring is Here When...

...you'd rather not wear the heavier coat since winter icicles axed of here spring.

...children don't make hugest snowman but preference styling on the beach builds of sand-dune.

...thrill in by the beach is beach, sand and soda all upgrading from stuck with in the house chores.

...there's a need for on a spring drive won't keep all in carseat from test humidity swift arrival.

...the family won't gripe this eager over field trip exempts from winter you stayed home.

...they can't shake an urge begins now for swift jogs around the park.

...mom is diligent with Monday start spring cleaning even if late finish is yet a few days.

...even the cat's eager bounding from windowsill for a quicky trek in less snow.

...your 12 year old inserted rather anxious of school almost out.

...the whole family validates put up with exercise the flab, gut and rear-end rather than 'too fat' next go at the beach.

You Know It's Time for Spring Cleaning when...

...after winter's passed things look moldy and cramped.

...a seeming vicious neighbor points out stubborn spot on dingy carpet.

...there's every urge to clear the hall closet of toys, suitcases and junk. But it won't do you start this minute.

...your child rejects play in a sour basement because of stacked up boxes and stale trunk's dusty.

...defective yard goods mar in living room drapes should have been swept clean merely eons ago.

...a distraught father can't find his fishing reel on the shelf same place he left it.

...you start Monday with clean in the kitchen shelves pots and pans but don't wind up with spring cleaning in the attic 'til goes on 2 days straight.

Odd Types of Memorandum

Dear mate,

In the final analysis one of us was wrong last evening. But always know I'll love you even so.

A forgiving wife.

Dear Jack,

Was it a Halloween treat or did you just happen to note I was out of orange candy dish?

A wife now owns a Halloween dish.

Dear mate,

I'm sure you'll love this present of a room humidifier. You've hinted times enough.

A husband with sharp ears.

Dear Larry,

I know you're hiding something because you bumble things lately. But did you have to spill punch last night and all over my boss's dinner jacket?

Your wife trying to snag a secret.

Dear hubby,

You certainly do remember dates but it's next week instead of next month's our Silver Anniversary.

Your wife who checks dates.

Dear mate,

A kiss for a treat is fun but don't come home without the Halloween candy you promised!

A wife loves candy besides.

Dear hubby,

I suppose you know I had furs, neighborhood garage and at parent's house mutt to boot. All that before we married. A wife anxious to ditch apartment for new home.

Dear mom,

In case you won't like the giant clown windsock I gave for a birthday present, I can always change it for Halloween mask is in season!

Your eight year old.

Dear Francine,

Your costume last night at Halloween's Ball was only made for you. You certainly do have Cat Woman's eyes.

A husband with eye for detail.

With the Child's Special Occasion for Say Grace

Easter Grace—Thanks for sending the Easter bunny filled my Easter basket. Now, I know I am a good girl afterall. Amen.

Tooth Fairy elation—Gee, I'm glad tooth fairy came last night. Now, I'm 5 years old and less one rotted link in chopper.

Birthday thanks—Wow! It's here again wads of ice cream, cake and gifts. Though the spacecraft present from dad, I think it's the best. Thanks.

Homecoming Blessing—God bless today a sis home from job too way out of town. Amen.

Recovery Grace—Thanks for mom's illness healed and in time to check a teenager's bad table manners.

Thanksgiving Grace—Gee, Gad! A feast is back big spread when parents don't have to tell me it's fun to eat. Even a 10 year old can amen!

Christmas delight—Christmas I cheer this bless my special parents chose the toys right won't cut me up or poison my liver insides. Amen.

You Know It's Reunion Time When…

…you're raring to go reunion but fear you don't know garbs to wear.

…you're not surprised last bent's on deep toner outfit you hope for a reunion less revealing.

…finally at Class Reunion you're glad they did turn to how changed Albana High looks and off who most successful not proned to be you.

…at any Class Reunion principal or a teacher still voiced full shouts where the stacked fruit and sandwich celebration except hairs receding bald are less full.

…if Class Reunion of '89 gets off "My how you've grown" to when other chats and dance in High School Auditorium, they fix date for next year.

…at any Family Reunion seems unfriendly if some relate on 'haven't been over since they moved to' is a bit way out.

…at swing Club Reunion the members think twice about noise upgrading this year over the last they joked and tuned of records played too loud.

…at any type reunion changes made can't be hidden.

After a Certain Age You Don't Fret as much

When you're Single and a Grandmother…

…you don't fret to serve the meals on schedule since it's just you to cook for.

…nobody will hint to you, "A lot of laundry." Single in your case it can pile up.

…you don't fret to clean behind 5 grandchildren seldom visit.

…over 50 if you fret about 400 calories in the parlor's banana shake, you know it settled in joint's thigh pocket.

…you don't have to appear in school's office because of your child's deeded mistake.

…since a free woman you don't worry about your mate was out late Sunday and watched tv sports all hours Monday.

…when your grandchildren do visit, you don't fret if they like play the video game. Unless they play it 12 hours.

…you don't swear if your date is just average—single and graying at the temples.

Denoting Facts On What's Inside The Surprise Pack

Beware the Minute Package

The classmate snoops of cased-in pouch only to be spooked by the quick pop up.

Down to-the-wire Achievement

Down to last 5 minutes term rates are read teenager frets 'til his teacher relates it out the bag 'B+'.

Suspicion put-to-the-Test

A moment when a Grammar teacher too curious of sack gift had to peep 'til 2 lash and golden oranges rolled out.

Mrs. Skeptic's Vigil–Point says

"Care before inspect of young donor's box. Well meaning donation could be live toad."

Miscellany not-in. Demand

Last moments inside Gift Shop lad had it packed polka dot tie over better looking shirt would have been in dad's favor.

Reluctant Shoe-in

Don't hope because a son's new elected High School Official he'd shoe mom in on surprise hat for her birthday.

Prerogative Up-Swing

The swing to raise thoughts to right gift for your daughter. She's a freshman, now.

It Depends On How Feelings Run When You Know

When she hates the yard sale item after turns brandy color pale, you know she picked wrong.

When she compared a rare vase at home with 4 mugs and 3 blunt artifacts now tucked in the shed, you know why she likes the vase.

When mom goes again one day for pairs of print slacks and yard sale tag from in the bunch, you know she enjoys a sale.

When the hubby not anxious takes the dim blade mower and hedge trimmer in to be shaved, you know he's hopes on infrequent discount.

You know he won't like inside the house taint perfuming 'smelly' than emp the junk.

About to shed a tear over my child the one drafted, you know you love him dearly.

Though sad because of graying pegs hair, what you realize into fortyish.

After waited so long for family on much needed vacation it's fun you understand forget cost is high.

When you felt good about Lunch truck came along, you know it's because of fruit drink special flavor.

Understanding Is You Kept Your Promise

When the wage earner didn't get scolded on the job he understands didn't mess up this week.

If you went from a fat 15 to size 10 you kept vow to lose weight.

If she kept Monday morning at in the attic, then at murky things in the basement, she kept promise in spring cleaning even if it took long.

Since it was your child lucked out almost on make the Track team you're glad she even had a goal.

If after all that 'burn off' looks are good in even jogging suit you're not fat as one time.

If twice a son didn't get ousted he must have played last half school's Basketball okay.

Since a boozer didn't take over one drink he understands how to kick booze.

If in the Lounge you wanted a third smoke but chewed gum instead you've not as yet kicked cigarettes but you take steps on the way.

If you weigh only two thirds fat on the scale at least you started groundwork.

Things You Recognize Since Your Luck Is Changing

You don't think a tan refrigerator looks out of place. You can set for kitchen makeover.

You see things clearly how to rid the lighter floor tiles' embedded scars. You next can pick browner pigment.

It's easy to believe luck had a hand in turning near chaos to house looking bliss after hubby got a raise last week. But it's hard believing spent it so fast.

When your child brings home average grades from school you don't hate the 2 C's.

When it's your neighbor gets the furniture piece of wood you can look jubilant for real.

You bring home bigger sacks meat, fruit, potatoes without next wish dollar power advanced more to your consumer buys giant size over teenie-weenie.

You don't take it personal for every little do-dads went wrong.

You stop buy news journal by quarterly. You can afford it by the month.

Shape you acknowledge in the mirror after lost a few pounds is you looking slimmer.

You don't. now wish good luck with eye venom because of her husband one promoted.

Autumn Months With School Year

A Student Quip

It's okay if parents know

In class I wrote the short essay.

But why is it parents have to know

Involves I didn't pass term year today?

Over-attentive Parent—The father at Open House showed a more than average interest in his child s teacher looked like.

Mrs. Sublime—The nice teacher in school.

September—When some mom's fed up can understand a 3 year-old head start right for Pre-school.

After sundown—When the class school teacher graded test papers for hours is glad no students around.

The Super Goofer—Student who goofs off in Social Studies too much to know of taxpayers about.

Bully Ambition—Not to bluff a child stands of 6 feet.

Astronaut too late—What a bully might become 10 years from now.

Things You Know About It's Thanksgiving

You know it's Thanksgiving when for certain it's your own small group kinfolk arrives.

You know for sure it's Thanksgiving when they on schedule. Few rather be late.

You know this year for Thanksgiving seating arrangements okay. Only one teen pouts about eat from young tot's instead of buffet's table.

You know comes with eat Thanksgiving turkey, dressing and rounds more dessert a kin gives the wishbone wish stated perfect.

You believe in short chats while we eat. Especially for Thanksgiving.

You know they won't stop ole granny this Thanksgiving either from she drinks overmuch spiked cranberry nog.

You don't know how but it's a blessing how this Thanksgiving same two relations don't argue.

You believe in everybody was satisfied this Thanksgiving after they all feasted to the full.

You Know It's Holiday Time When...

...Labor Day—If there's a big parade missed, you're too busy getting burned in back yard with fire the grill.

...Thanksgiving—You watch more Tv marathon with your family after get stuffed on some turkey thigh and trimmings if you can still sit up that long.

...two weeks before Christmas—You're way ahead with tree decorations hung. And candy canes and edge trims make you anxious behind mad weeks ahead search was in Department Store crowds.

...on Christmas—Each family member's too happy for the one gift from grab bag so week after Christmas less for goes back to store—item some mismatch big or small.

...on New Years—You long to watch Tv but can't tear your husband from watch of something fames flowers or fruit bowl.

...behind New Years—You look for what's next—Holiday on the calendar.

Knowing Your Kins and Relations

The mom always knows the auntie hands over trinket even after my child was bad.

Niece here adores the favorite auntie brings me what-nots and wood artifacts from the yard sale. But hate "I can't use a clown too huge for my shelf's menagerie."

I'm not surprised if one bearded uncle rather donate his old car wheel, record warp and tapes to friend's garage sale than rather scrap all for junk.

You dread if one mother-in-law "won't let me down gently" if failed arranging silk flowers.

You don't despite the young cousin hunts to achieve at piccolo playing. Long as he won't play it overloud in my house.

There's always fear of young kin may explore too much before nabbed owes to child did tip every bit of china vase and bought piece from display in my window.

You Know For Certain It's Winter When…

…dad hates to use the snow plough more than once a month.

…lazy mutt yelps to go out but whines too much if bitten by 'It's cold'.

…mom won't have spring cleaning but spends too much time with winter clean muddy rug if whoever missed a doormat.

…looking forward to Christmas is easy though just getting over a cool Halloween and Thanksgiving.

…you don't go to winter Carnival or Fair 'til way after big snow subsided better.

…even cat in windowsill figures best just stare out some days.

…Christmas is right around the corner and already about the tree these ornaments' decorations.

…you don't Know what do about dirty sneakers and boots except pile all in the bathroom.

Putting The Grin Between You And Me

by

Annette Stovall

If We Could Have The Wishes We've Always Wanted...

...I'd have strawberry colored bathtub instead of white.

...you'd have more than one tan kitchen appliances hide blot and I'd have perfect hair.

...the demonstrator would make it work removing 1 part gravy stain, 2 cups coffee and 1 berry crimson float from store rug—and we'd get the stain out at home always.

...if the fortune card said "Due for what's super" it would always be money.

...if you'd wish for what's costly you've wanted, it could be nice to hear "We at last own the home."

...I'd be so creative I'd only get compliments.

...I'd have that. pleasurable trip always wanted and make a wish in public there would be a public vendor with run on fruit drinks.

...from their holiday gift list we'd only receive right gift always.

...you'd donate item to charity and would get something back—credit on your tax sheet.

...I'd have 9 pairs of shoes in line always.

...plastic surgery would never cost that much.

If I Could Make the Much Needed Changes...

…I'd change in the kitchen, cabinets from same ole dull to new in tan.

…I'd have permed hair would out-last cooking in sweat!

…there'd be no such day as Friday the 13th!

…when guests would arrive, I wouldn't have to explain why I need to get the bathroom 'classic leak' fixed. Instead it would be.

…I'd say, this year, definitely, "Going on a trip" instead of 'maybe.'

…I'd go 'coach' or 'class' any vacation without fear of flying.

…first sign of couch fade I'd have to change it in the store for `trade off.'

…there'd be no such thing as got the 'note' overdrawn. Just a filled in bank book!

…I'd have 'gourmet meal' beknown to class restaurant served any day now at home, instead of wait the occasion.

Since We Do and Say a Certain Thing—It Won't Be Just Right

Standing on the corner early morning for a bus comes late—it won't be a pleasant wait.

Searching the block again for best ole ancient age—it won't be a house special like before.

To agree the oversized loan to a friend is personal—but it won't be sensible receiving no words in writing.

Saying, "I'll turn the E Bond in"—it won't be redeemed 'til after 30 more years.

A husband may promise say, "I'll start on diaper baby and clothes in the hamper"—but it won't be time begin starts this early morning.

Sitting on parental right to take the family on vacation in July—later won't be 'soon' as family hoped.

To go to auction and next not make bid on government owner-ships—it won't be likely house and lot in mind.

Trying for government loan may get you somewhere—but it won't be next week.

There's No Surprise If...

...your tot takes mealtime for clamor toy time.

...mom shops for Supermarket quality baby food in medium, fine or table just to have your child's fuss rejects 3 vegetables.

...your child clamors deep grimace over put away the toys big racket. Thinks no fair.

...what you kick on gained 2 gray hairs is a Middle Age Crisis.

...two figure won't get somewhere with price up in our area unless boat, great Refigerator and child's Gym something to show for.

...after mate's on commission in with scimpiest net wage, you think of who's on welfare not that bad off.

...marrieds think twice about twice buy Government bonds if can't cash one in, faced with noisy sink grind.

...you figure you won't stop adding gray hair 'til stop adding on children.

It Could Be A Nice Trick…

…if the child wouldn't have off days and disobey after say, "I'll be good."

…if each time weatherman's forecast of mellow sunshine, shine we wouldn't frown on next we under graying clouds.

…if the child wouldn't get sick put you in the 'poor-house.'

…if you wouldn't get the overdrawn bank note disables credit cards.

…if you'd never get a headache over brought one tent, jug and gear 'phernalia but left a camp stove major need, but at home.

…if you'd never feel anxious over Beauty Parlor or Masseuse will have to wait the turn.

…if age would have added you 3 more graying fade hairs than needed, but you won't think much of.

…if you'd feel less for miserable over gained 5 pounds.

…if gadget's gizmo bought at yard sale, fully operative.

if skin needs 'mud pack' or else Health Spa's whole entire assembly.

It Could Be A Nice Trick…

…if in the "kitchen floor tiles remained nice shine after current rainy spell.

…if the tub in the bathroom was a nice shade of pink.

…if the toast never burned a nice shade of charcoal.

…if the dark suit you wear Committee group night won't just hide the fat but get the nice member off your age.

…if you don't hesitate to give the prankster for a friend a nice doosy of a birthday present.

…if you don't feel bad over your child's not nice at Banquet social.

…if the Brownie Club meet never held it on 'full moon' night. A nice leader might next have a mood swing.

…if you remember tip the cab driver got you through a traffic jam in one piece. It was a nice gesture.

…if gadget's gizmo turned out a nice heirloom.

How Feelings Ran If We Neglected Do And Say Some Things

We felt bad especial about shop so long if dirty chore we put off still waits at home.

We could have kicked ourselves for let the paint dingy bathroom go.

You didn't feel anything eccentric of let the mate start out. for 6 plasterboards, paste and 2 dozen nails when you forgot 'a holiday.'

You felt guilty over not say definitely you wanted darker color hair tint last trip in the shop.

You didn't feel bad of no 'yes' to son was too young for driver's license.

We felt deranged for not add specifics in doctor's office when we had to go a second trip for blood and lab samples cost extra.

We felt a let down if door sign's '10 to 5' we thought would open earlier.

You didn't feel sick over didn't denote a parking sign's 'between 2 and 5' 'til after fine cost plenty.

You felt bad about not say graphics on government claim delivered check this late.

What A Different Note Would Say

Dear mate,

Give a little. If you only knew how I feel when you hide behind the newspaper 8p.m. every night.

From a loving wife.

Dear Jack,

This is just a memo on married couples need notes to each other. I know since I read it here in the latest magazine.

From Ann

Dear Honey,

You do deserve credit. Though you don't need constant reminding how you bake 3 great pies at once, can things besides lay 7 pairs of socks neatly arranged in the drawer.

Hubby Mel

Dear mate,

Thanks again for the ring. Only don't be 2 years replacing it if the doctor prys it up again!

Truly a larger wife.

Dear wife,

I put up with a lot. But did you have to cut in with books you've read! Although my factory boss last night seemed okay.

Hubby David

Dear Romeo,

It's funny I call you that since I'm complaining now. Did you have to spend all last evening watching tv football?

Sincerely Audrey

According to He Says...It Means

If he says...

"I didn't say gymnastics."

It means...

He won't like to admit his mistake.

If he says...

"Of course, there's always another day for biceps."

It means...

He minds of say he's overweight.

If he says...

"Besides, these newspaper ads could be in bolder print."

It means...

He's the main one needs glasses.

If he says...

"Of course, small type none too easy reading."

It means...

He thinks you don't have knowledge beside small newspaper type, important route map and appendage label—too he none astute eye.

If he says...

"The ink should be another color. So I'm blind."

It means…

He'd rather admit to color blind than say he didn't have a label straight.

If he says…

"Why should I seek directions anyhow?"

It means…

You're out on highway route number and he's

If he says…

"The baked Alaskan salmon tastes heavenly. What's derelict about service?"

It means…

He thinks of restaurant entree 'grand' while they need one other waitress handy at least.

If he says…

"In fact, you look superb that size. You don't need it."

It mean

He won't agree to you enroll in Weight Salon just for lose 2 sizes down. S…

If he says…

"How much can a lounger jacket inflate?"

It mean…

He wishes he did pump weights earlier, maybe.

According to She Says...It means

If she says...
"Of course, class is out."

It means...
She just got in from school.

If she says...
"Of course, you still do look beat."

It means...
He's in his lounging chair and wearing shoes untied.

If she says...
"Today we did scientific study on astronauts in space."

It means...
She doesn't want him to fall asleep on how they manage sip food and box drinks with a straw while drifting weightless.

If she says...
"You don't mean to say that. Do you?"

It means...
He didn't give right answer on women walk the moon or something.

If she says...
"Dear, you don't really intend remain slouched."

It means…

He needs to sit up straight in chair he lounging in when the Brownie Club's due any minute.

If she says…

"Why try and hide the job gave you sick leave?"

It means…

He's embarrassed by the child asked.

If she says…

"Of course, I do need to learn a trade."

It means…

To her study Lab Techniques unlike stay at home and mend of shabby socks ripped holes.

If she says…

"Of course, you could have watched him more. He was already buckled."

It means…

He wasn't careful with junior tipped over jams and jellies in the aisle with stroller along mother shopped.

If she says…

"It's just weekend in Cicero. Not like trip to the moon or something."

It means…

They don't take vacations enough.

If We'd Have Taken Our Own Advice...

…I'd have schedule for everything.

…I'd have stuck with leave note to Ralph saying, "Pick up suit from Dry Cleaners."

…you wouldn't have planned on 8 Brownie girls track mud in. Next rainy meet you'll have 'em each set pair of shoes beside doorway first off.

…you wouldn't have up front told your teenager "Maroon jersey faded."

…I'd have kept tab's memorandum on where misplaced item above else achieved 'missing.'

…you would have roasted orange cuts give the house a sweeter smell first before 1p.m. list came—6 orderly members from local branch.

…we would have said it out, "I'll take the needed vacation this year."

…I'd have random memorabilia on tabs always.

…I would have saved face with bring rainscarf along no matter how bright sun at first

…you would have planned on 5p.m. with dinner guests—take the bad jokes too.

It Could Be Trick Or Not...

...if the recuperating aunt didn't say thanks on the phone for the card. Or else you mailed it late.

...if your hair won't stay of gussied up in public.

...if in the yard sale you bought a fancy artifact thing you don't need. Or else in the living room no place for display.

...the sick child could be faking because of no A in class on Foreign Histology Types.

...the dressmaker explaining you said twice as many inches off. Or else you told her wrong.

...when the public scale revealed weight shifted by over 3 pounds. You could have sworn your not 130.

...you think the plumber's totals for chalk line drains too much. Or else you don't keep up with chalk weight, drains and price change.

...you need weight equipment or else don't need pricing Aerobics class.

...if you pinched over an inch of flab try a Fat Salon.

The Year In Summer Was Here, You Remember What You Said...

…"It's hot" while hand of artifact thing to garage sales-clerk.

…"Those are not my kittens wandered in" to cross the fence inquiring neighbor.

…a dad said he'd take all to Big Bear Mountain to see every animal visible this year didn't lose nerve.

…angry words to gained of stormy grounds on weirder yardfest.

…congradulative words to 9 year-old now little league star.

…they all said they wanted more soda at team league's yard in pleasant social.

…in the Department Store you said "The thin brown out-fit should be cooler" for year you under vivid rays.

…the family all promised this summer they'd curve on overspend credit cards and said later "We did almost."

Dealing With Trick Question It Depends

To answer where do babies come from it depends on how you word it.

In order answer strange question why 3 puppies colored hazel it depends on should you know puppy pedigree.

You won't like the conversation led into, "Changed hair-styles" if it depends on should you say, "Dyed."

You won't want to answer your husband's "cost was how much?" if depends on how to say chairs and 2 couches, redesigned tapestry put squeeze on credit cards.

If you answer awkward to 'if sable coat real,' it depends on being a fake.

If you don't speak up to 'so many splendid darker kittens in the bunch,' it depends on what you know of cat biology.

When you answer a friend, yes, the suit bought new when it's used, it depends on how you bought it from the Salvation Army.

Recognizing Mood Is Now In High Gear...

...you won't mind clouds in overhang shaded dark.

...you won't mind curly perm blows disorderly the ride home.

...you'll mind 2 chairs and couch look dingy faded in the room but won't remodel right away.

...you won't mind your husband gone to the ball game with a friend. You'll think a subtle thought.

...you won't mind letting friend in on naughty secret if she will keep it.

...you won't mind the tv is programmed dull. It'll have to play better.

...you won't mind looking prettier than fat. You will rather be happy with flatter yourself.

...you'll mind getting the same store duns every twice a month. Though in your heart consoling, you won't crack up.

...you won't mind if the weatherman's 'cast of dark storm shoots wild is a mistake. You will love here's milder breeze better.

Is It Being Cheap or Just Playing it Safe...

...if you automatically ask for joint bank account because it's safer now that no secret withdraws.

...if you systematically recycle plastic anything because you later find what else they're useful for.

...anytime being consistent about the mate wear blue attires to the function, because it's cheap or safe than wear the beige next needs cleaning.

...if you admit you buy stockpile because any ordinary day better prices could change.

...anytime a couple ceeds to boss's wife split the bill because it saves when dining ala carte.

...if it became customary buying the cheaper brand because stove gets dirty again anyway.

...anytime being urgent on take the child bike out of repairs on time because you know those rates.

...if you immediately buy the cut rate pass, because it's easy knowing ahead rides on bus fares next accelerate up.

When We Fame—To Avoid Pitfalls...

...sitting anywhere in public smoke house is not okay 'til after we realize mistake made leads to no smoke's zone.

...driving without a license unpermitted especially to sixteen year old youngster.

...anytime we don't relish a friend's 3rd draft we know it's because of 'over drinks too much.'

...trying to stretch ends meet on net wage is average unless pig and pan low stretched 'til we have to any seek welfare.

...anybody jumps in head of crowd standing in the Super-Market line is not right. Still they have to be told where's the long line's end.

...circling the block again for where park is expected over caught where sign expressed 'between 3 and 7.'

...each time we buy the newspaper it's because we know look for deals on Super Discount or Personal ad.

On Thanksgiving Fact Is You Can't Resist…

…in fact seating the umpteen members at the table. But to say they don't look squeezed in ranks in understatement.

…chiding your uncles's 3 tads next. No problem for the uncle looks on.

…in fact you love showing off to members the new gravy dish and scoop ladle for Thanksgiving—the manufacturer's along with new china.

…you won't okay again this year your teen who looses zip over sit with smaller tads.

…in fact you hope your favorite auntie makes the wishbone wish fast so we can keep gorging on turkey, dressing, and pie.

…saying 'thanks' a hostess didn't need to out of pocket for gift giving. A few brought you present instead.

…in fact you love laying down the law, "Don't smoke in the house."

…after delicious meal enjoy the calm 'til same 2 certain relations argue.

…by eve you have to then and there try on the 'sweats' gift in fact gets you arm lengths too short or too long.

…saying "Thanksgiving only comes once a year is a fact."

Things We Wouldn't' Conceive Of Be Without Unless

We wouldn't conceive of go without a washer unless—it broke.

We wouldn't conceive of be without a microwave oven unless—we can't afford to buy one.

We wouldn't think of no skillet, pot or pan of our own unless—we live with our folks and use theirs.

You wouldn't dream of no tv near vicinity when busy in the kitchen unless—they took your favorite soap off.

You wouldn't conceive of tv without remote control or push buttons unless—your set was coming back from 'in shop' soon.

We wouldn't think of be without a dust buster unless dirt we rummage out is easy get at.

We'd never conceive of be without bag linings for trash, hamper or rag pile unless we project, "We shop soon."

We wouldn't conceive of go without nest of plastic bags and foil unless like people on welfare—we have enough stored up.

'Remembering' Brings The Humor Back

by

Annette Stovall

Things We Kicked About Remembering Back

We kicked about no coppertone refrigerator in better kitchen.

We kicked about lighter floor tiles never kept sheen appearance.

You kicked about not losing much in Weight Salon.

You kicked about Beauty Parlor didn't get all the wrong tint out.

We kicked about our mate didn't buy a great washing machine 'til now a rinse cycle beyond repairs. Then he had to.

You kicked about kitchen stove never tan.

We kicked about Bank Accounts, Credit Cards or Mortgage if overdrawn by mega-dollars much.

We kicked about vending machine didn't work. Then we kicked it.

We kicked about having to seek Welfare 'til our first big check came was lump sum. Then we later kicked again.

We kicked about standing on cold corner for late bus arrives.

You kicked about kids disarrayed the attic.

You kicked about let manicure wait.

Brief Remembrances Of She Was Even Single And On The Ornamental Date

She remembers in the doorway date was shy but she managed smile behind one rose he gave.

In ornamental card about her she couldn't believe so many gorgeous words.

On a first date even mattered if he said "You look undeniably pretty."

Her first night dancing on ballroom ornamental tiles shimmer, they were having big fun since she had to be reminded how fast the time went.

Reminiscing reminds how it was single on the arm beau in style—it was worth every minute.

If he wore the slick ornamental boots and tie had zip—all next added tang to sophisticated concert.

Last date was on a balcony under silvery ornamental moon when he complimented her eyes she didn't believe she blushed for girl of 20 odds.

If no hard shut door on his latter advances, she remembers liked the ornamental eve.

Remembering Back to When It Was a Lovely Evening

Last week they reminisced, it was lovely evening 'til he had to go home.

She still recalls 'After 5 Eve' was lovely but he wore the wrong slacks.

Even mom's reminded she had a good time Class Reunion Eve though she did spill the strawberry punch and cake icing on a real new dress.

A cousin out of school still names Fulton High was Fun Eve late Pageant out in open.

Chats a year ago between chums vent lovely evening when 2 didn't argue.

Not long ago you spent a lovely 3 hours ride on Amtrak because of 'shouldn't take long.'

Even dad recalls mood was sti31 'relax' though the eve he finally turned down for a raise didn't reflect on Christmas Bonus.

It was a lovely afternoon even with the knowledge 3 Government E Bonds don't mature in 5 years.

The last time 2 caught a Famous Class Act it was a lovely evening. Two yet reminisce.

Remembering When It Was Good Day For Spring Cleaning...

...forecast was only warm for late March.

...It was good day for Glass Plus.

...you hasted cleared the closets of 'cram' shoes, toys or clothes needed 'donate' rather than trash stockpile.

...fancy drapes were just begging to be hung.

...neighbor's brief interchange didn't venture of "Table sheen's bit smudgy."

...Mr. Clean had the ultimate test on grime anything.

...you rearranged few items an hall shelf without misplace of value hubby's reel and tackle.

...musty smell in the attic just had to be sprayed.

...you couldn't waste a minute going without toss accumulated rags from in the cellar rather than let junk pile up.

What I Remember About Shoes Now and Back Then

A month ago a shoe was perfect fit not until step into store pairs nearly 20.

Since being grown I remember dirty buckskins special for Grammar School or track mud on linoleum in the kitchen.

I remember High School dance not that hot not without wear the slickest patent leather or suede pumps.

Back then a sore mom put doubt to rest with, "If the shoe fits wear it."

Next as young mother with my own best children—like me they wore the shameful rubber boots not until 'snowed that much' in near zero weather.

After beyond early age, I couldn't see how 'wore the now Status building Pump' participated in High School Pageant.

Next into Middle age, Platform shoes, Spike heels and tall stairs I take or leave.

Now nearing Senior, I agree with a grandmother says ever so emphatically, "Give me street shoe of greatly comfort."

Remembering Back to When We Missed a Tip or Almost

If last week a child missed hearing "Tip lightly" mom's cake maybe flattened.

Last year on vacation if an angry dad by his family missed or almost didn't tip, the porter must had the suitcases wrong.

If one bright afternoon on the walk a mate was slow of tip hat, an in-law did deride he's bald.

If Brownie Club leader mom didn't tip at restaurant, all worst entree horrible.

Last vacation you tipped a sad cabbie 20 cents down from your customary 10 percent, he didn't say 'Thanks' or else did with a frown.

If one dark holiday night a late pair missed tip politely in from Ballroom Celebration, they woke 3 nosy tads and baby-sitter squeaked.

If only a month ago you missed tip public scale over, you didn't gain 8 pounds.

Odd Types of Memorandum

Dear Jake,

It was a comfort last night just to chat rather than just watch television.

Your loving wife.

Dear Parents,

Thought you'd like to know this morning our neighbor's cat had 3 adorable kittens need a home, I hope.

Your daughter

Dear Mom,

I just broke your 2 whatnots, a swedish doll from prize collection and skipped go to class today.

From your son on April Pool's Day!

P.S. Did I fool you?

Dear Folks,

If you wish to get me something special for my birthday, don't be naive just do.

Your 10 year old.

Dear Hubby,

Please don't eat the 3 dozen cookies in the 'frig. I made 'em especial for the Brownie Club Meet.

Your mate

Dear Mom,

Since Mother's Day this Sunday I vow to never again throw dirty sneakers and socks in my closet for you pick up.

Your 12 year old.

Dear Dad,

I'm sorry my pet frog gift didn't please you for Father's Day

Your 5 year old

Since Reached Middle Age You Don't Always Like To Be Reminded Of...

…how you once were that age, after just looking at young friend in the market.

…how you added of another middle-age wrinkle.

…how most high-paying jobs for youngster with hard drive and urges none of which fit your fortyish years.

…you can't see to understand job ads without Contac-lens or glasses.

…you added another stale graying hair-strand.

…on the dance floor you can't exaggerate dance or move swift than your daughter.

…you have that many 8 grandchildren.

…in the stores that that color lipstick on your skin's turning darker, how it's too bright for your age.

…on job interviews, how old all your 5 children.

…how in Weight Salon person lost most in one week, not me.

…how you could use professional in-shop manicure or fake nails.

Occasions We Hate To Remember but Still Do

I hate to remember sitting in the Clinic all day, but still do.

I hate to remember standing in the Supermarket line was long even without a July 4th near.

We hate to remember we walked 6 blocks in the rain before a Public Transportation in sight.

We hate to remember occasion for a do-it-yourself kit wouldn't do without add a friend's Philips driver, 3 bolts and nuts not included and 2 sore thumbs.

We hate to remember Holiday celebration went wrong but still do.

I hate to recall of a clinic 'took a catscan.'

You can't help but recall occasion when your household of 5 almost in the bread line because of credit cards over-drawn by 400 dollars.

We hate to remember when we had to seek Welfare, but still do.

Remembering When It Was A Good Week for Campout...

...they didn't fret about the weather on average was nice.

...2 children didn't fight about who'd fill the water jugs.

...mom didn't have fit over 'brought a camp stove, 2 big jugs and dozen or so tins were handy but left a can opener at home.'

...the child didn't of convenience get lost from the tent.

...mom didn't become upset because felt a little rain day one with campout.

...dad with his son didn't go near the frame abandoned house and not find in the woods rocks were useful for prop a leaning camp stove.

...dad didn't lose his cool over 5th day with camp-out his fishing tackle broke.

...week ended, the family didn't leave with a feeling they wouldn't like pitch here again in Camp Village next year.

Time Out for Prior Contrasts

I still Remember…

…as a youngster time I had with dance for hours—a fun party.

…a time when asked to dance only once recollects a dull party.

…the year I said I was 40 wasn't bad since ideals only thirty five.

…fond recall on how in Grammar School I cut the back out from shirt I thought on pattern's fold but mistake made was on selvage instead.

…one Albana Grade School teacher with pleasant name but mammoth the shout in class.

…one neighbor had rowdy tot though handsome fee paid for 'I babysit.'

…young age when not a dentist tongs but wood bat mistake dropped a tooth.

…perhaps one old neighborhood was good therapy after all, because 'Hide and Seek' just turned into 'Chase and Court.'

I Remember When It was A Good Spring Season

And just for Acknowledge Spring…

…I placed a pair of scuffed winter shoes and heavy gloves tucked early season.

…I skipped a dull cleaning chore at home for walks test humidity seasonal.

…where the children paddled fantasy oars in back yard, I took the imagined boat ride in fun no apparent mean reason.

…when a store clerk said, "Next," I replaced seasonal winter coat with spring jacket finer light.

…brief walks on the block I wondered of me with no raised nmbre11a for shade same am folk some hot

…day at the beach wasn't ended without at least bring home few exotic burnt sea shells for display.

…on the spring drive at landscape I didn't miss of precious moment however seasonal.

…I took a brief rest period in the interim when spring cleaning next awarded me burn out.

The Average Complaints You Don't Need To Be Reminded Of Seeing is Believing...

...how he could be charming on a date like when you first met.

...when you go diversion theatre he minds holding hands.

...he's a mite terrific father 'til he sleeps just lounging around in his old lounging pajamas.

...how he turns a deaf ear to serious interchanging talks prolong about.

...he compares you to his mother.

...you mind performing bulk of house chores.

...when he's asked to move the junk bag, 2 chairs and end table, you don't expect hearing him say "Later."

...when you want a quiet romantic evening, you don't mean in front of tv watching football.

Picks On Wartime Do's and Don'ts

Don't speak about the Trench—Although it was ridiculous how in combat he saw the fresh crud hole but missed the wide trench!

Don't say Daydream—Shush, about how he so busy 'dreaming of back home he didn't hear a charge say "Forward."

On his 'Pees and Ques'—Fatherly chats with a son it's okay to glory in ripped a 'Fascist Pig' but quiet on 'met the girls at Waikiki Beach.'

A cleared Conscience—A post-wartime militia man admits

"During wartime, yes, I failed with study Demographics."

Don't doubt a lonely War Bride—It's okay to say, now, how it was, then, in Army Camp.

Do tell of Purple Heart—Near triumphs he brags about how 'won a Purple Heart—almost.'

Do tell of an Ending—It's okay for a once G.I. becomes turned 'Jap Jive' to Peace Treaty.

Odd Types of Memorandum

To a late riser,

I hope you liked breakfast. I fixed it rather than not eat.

An early husband.

Dear Ned,

For sake of household of 6 you do grand. Except you don't emp the trash without a wife's prompting.

A caring wife.

Dear Parents,

Here's reminder birthday is coming up soon.

From who wants a gift.

Dear Mom and Pop,

I didn't do well this year on test grades, I don't know from where I've acquired slow genes. Was it you?

From your school age daughter who wonders.

To Henry,

Here's a list reminding to pick up the groceries, 6 mugs and a tumbler. And don't just meet up with the guys in the bar like last evening.

A waiting wife.

To a Darling Family,

I like I got favorite presents this year. All fit rights except the trunks.

From a Father's Day dad.

To Dear Parents,

If you may okay a driver's license I'll sweat and ponder along 'To get A's.' Two things I didn't do last school year's term.

Anticipation's son.

The Dope On School Year In Memorandum

Memorandum Stint—The child keeps a diary meant for next dope on blackball the stereotyped event.

Note Resolve—One A student won't pass note in class if it won't lead to get 'credits' for.

First-hand-Dispatch—A lapped up report on Classroom Enhancements a P.T.A. clan gets ahead of others find out.

Events-Fun-Schedule—List for 'going' teenager in High School hopes parents will agree.

Median Position—No base for principal undecided on P.T.A. demands.

Scribble a Letter—One dad discovers here, fast, at P.T.A.'s no place for.

Best term-Directive—Speeding through High School homework's no authentic way upgrade the year in term data.

Best Slang—The longest run paper in school nicknamed a Greek.

This year's Record Event—How tall Vera is. A friend wonders of why she never kept intrinsic records on 'how tall' in gym suit before.

Memorandum Scoop—About gym no written exams.

Some Things We Kicked About Back Then

Remembering back to School days…

…we kicked about tote over many books to school.

…we kicked on walk to school cold days. Now our own children ride. At least sometimes.

…you kicked when no lunch money for school. Now your child gets an extra nickel sometimes.

…a sore mom kicked of got a C card or rotten term paper same as we do with our children.

…after Grammar School principal kicked on 'spilled the lunch bucket sandwich in schoolmate's hair,' you did and still do kick resulting punishment.

…before a school teacher kicked on 'brought 2 bananas, all at home, instead of apple and an orange to Class Party,' you regret now you kicked to parents.

…you kicked when a sibling started Pre-school first, when mom with crying about it.

…we kicked if missed a High School Track or Football game same as son just kicked.

…we kicked if go to High School Prom in 'that ole gown' same as our daughter kicked.

Remembering Time Was For The Rest Period

Tender year's Rhyme

The book delayed of student is apt

And point on Social Studies catches draft

It comes on outdoor games address

We glad for now the recess

Quick Discovery was

In gym they never would credit clever write-ups but clever leisure.

Immaterial High School Match

Archaic in High School rest period, ethereal was they ended featherweight homework 'clock time' best than who off sick didn't have a care.

Delabored Pause

De-animated interval concerted at home not refreshing without spend the half hour in sip coffee.

Slumber Guard

Distraught as straining winter nights with guard the AC,DC wool from one's mate was fair protocol.

Juvenile Quest

Did the President ever take a rest from 'Neutra-Ban-Conference.'

Year '50's Artifice

No assassins near miss was a damper on Secret Service.

When Sleep Time Become The Jester

Geometry Sleepihead

One school-age boy put to sleep on Geometry books but popped eyelids when teacher's tease called out, "Sex!"

Night Owl at Home

One dozing 15 year-old would always flunk school test until she found arraigning culprit in night-owl Pop music.

In-bed-with Spouse Option

That night her ears ticked to he flaps the newspaper Journal.

Wide-Awake-Druthers

The more his little brother tuned to take a nap, the more he'd rather 'instigated else than homework.'

Old Jake's Logic

"Too much talk about sleep won't slumber it next landed Mrs. Dalton Insomnia."

Slumber Alternative

Torpor's mother was glad when her daughter's pajama party was cancelled to family slept like a top because of rain storm.

Father Rationale

A dad reasoned if he watched the game 'til Saturday night late, he'd next sleep through Pastor James Long Sunday sermon.

Remembering A Class Reunion When Ambitions Mostly Talked

The graduated class of '87…here reunited still had ambitious, goals and fun.

After they brought the fruits, cookies and cake on the table, they still talked of ambitions must be achieved.

Before they had fun with dancing the most famous gave a speech not overdramatized for some had top drives.

After chatted with favorite teacher gave you drive in '87, you didn't know back then when flustered he had visions of become official Lunar Astro.

The High school cheerleader wondered out loud of Desk Clerk leads to Media Announcer.

Meanwhile, least likely to succeed was doing fine with play best piano in the room.

Beneath a flow of streamers and balloons a few had fun with play checkers amid talk of serious drives for better future.

Above an ending, talk was on bring to next year's reunion better goals came true than in this year discussed on.

Remembering When It Was Booming Day For Sale...

...you bought 2 choice artifacts of Yard sale not before check for 'Hand made' on the base.

...sun was beaming on the Sidewalk sale had clothes you couldn't pass up.

...you thrilled to rummage of small appliances, bikes and tvs Garage sale. Then decided on bike horn best for 10 year old.

...it was an ideal day for 'Made in the U.S.A.' and 'Union' tags.

...after picked a half dozen tins of pet food, you couldn't neglect detergent and fine item on sale though a hungry cat awaited dinner at home.

...you wanted stop at Discount Store nearby. Then reminded you had 'that brand' handy on the shelf already.

...last stop was Hardware Store for hose. Now with packed car and sun going down, more convenient items on sale had to wait for other sale days.

Odd Types of Memorandum

Dear John,

Everytime subject of money comes up why do you win and I lose?

A puzzled wife.

Dear mate,

This is a note to say this time my mother can't be blamed for I'm on a big shopping spree away from chores.

Distraught wife.

To a late sleeper,

I went ahead with breakfast anyway even though it turned out burned.

Your loving husband.

To Dad,

I found an old baby picture of you in the attic. Didn't they wear clothes in those days?

Your 8 year old.

Dear Phil,

Since you kick overspending I'm giving you something simple for Valentine's Day. A red card.

Your mate

Dear mate,

This is just reminder in plenty of time, your mother-in-law'll be over for Labor Day—all day.

Your hubby

To my Husband,

I neglected say last night since knowing you'd mind reopened of 500 dollar old charge yesterday.

Your mate

To Mom,

I hope you liked my present of one earring. Dad bought you the other one.

Your 6 year old.

Odd Types of Memorandum

Dear Henry,

This reminder, we have our own anniversary to go to in just 5 days.

Your darling wife.

Dear mate,

If you want to keep the peace don't forget we're due to help out at fundraiser this evening.

Wife Ann

To my mom,

A heart shaped card and a kiss are all I have to give you that's special on Valentine's Day.

From your 9 year old son.

Dear parents,

Thanks. It was the surprise birthday party I hadn't had in 5 years.

Your 15 year old daughter.

To my darling wife,

This is noteworthy to say on Valentine's Day, I never dreamed we'd be that happy. Almost like 10 years ago!

Hubby Ralph

Dear Jim,

Thanks for the candy. We should have a type of fairy tale gift giving even when it's not a holiday!

Wife Mable

To My 2 Parents,

I'm running away from home to join the Brownie Club. But I'll be back before nightfall.

Your 7 year old.

About the Author

She was born in St. Louis Missouri and now lives in California. She's had works published in several anthologies and has submitted works to different publications. She has written works since 1978.